SELECTED POEMS OF TAKAGI KYOZO

Selected Poems
of
Takagi Kyozo

introduced and translated by James Kirkup and Michio Nakano

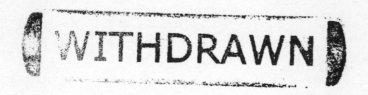

A CARCANET PRESS PUBLICATION

SBN 85635 067 2

First published 1973
by Carcanet Press Limited
266 Councillor Lane
Cheadle Hulme
Cheadle, Cheshire

Printed in Great Britain
by W & J Mackay Limited, Chatham

Contents

Introduction

AMONG MODERN Japanese poets Takagi Kyozo is unique for two reasons. In the first place, he has succeeded in using dialect in a most evocative and poetic way. His dialect is the Tsugaru dialect, one of the dialects of Tohoku. It is spoken in Aomori Prefecture, in the region facing the Japan Sea.

Some poets have occasionally attempted to write poems partly in dialect, in order to obtain a regional atmosphere. Takagi is unique in that his poems are often written *entirely* in the Tsugaru dialect. If a Japanese whose native dialect is not that of Tohoku hears one of Takagi's poems, he will not be able to understand it at all. But if he reads the text of the poem, he will understand it to a certain extent, aided by *kanji* or ideographs.

Thus he can appreciate some of the beauty of the sounds in Takagi's poems. This is one of the secrets of Takagi's success. Of course, the *kanji* are not used just to communicate meanings to readers. The Japanese language is ordinarily written in a mixture of *kanji* and *kana*, though generally only one form is used in any one word. Poets are very careful in deciding whether a word should be written in *kanji* or in *kana*, just as English poets discriminate between Latin and Anglo-Saxon forms or between the use of capital and lower-case letters. This suggests that in Japanese poetry the appeal to the eye is a very important element.

In the second place, Takagi Kyozo is unique in that he expects his poems to be read aloud, though Japan is not a land of poetry readings and poets rarely recite their works in public. But Takagi is an exception. In his latest edition of *The Winter Moon* (the original title is *Marmelo* [Tsugaru Shobo, Aomori, 1967]), he provides the reader with a phonosheet on which three poems from the collection are read by himself. He also holds poetry readings on occasions. Though a non-Tohoku Japanese will not understand these readings, he will be able to appreciate their strange beauty if he takes the trouble to read the texts before listening to the recordings. He can also enjoy the recordings in a purely musical way, because of the poet's style of reading.

However, Takagi's poems are unique not only for these reasons. The fact that these poems when translated into English retain much of their original beauty tells us that they possess other qualities. They express the feelings of a strong, bitter yet delicate and sensitive personality, and well reflect the harsh surroundings in which he was brought up. He gives us scenes of ordinary, plain, unvarnished Japanese life, an austere life of savage hardship and patient toil which is in direct contrast to the lives of

7

most Japanese today. Takagi uses simple, earthy, direct but colourful words to express a variety of universal human emotions. This must be the essential secret of the appeal in Takagi's poetry.

In translating these poems, we have tried to keep as close to the original as possible. James Kirkup, coming from a similarly harsh and cold environment in the north of England, and for several years resident in the Tohoku area, has tried to convey the spareness of style and imagery and the picturesque language without burdening it with northern English dialect expressions, which might be just as incomprehensible to the English reader as Takagi's Japanese is to the ordinary Japanese. We have not tried to make these poems say more than they do in the originals: that is, we have refused to intellectualize them or to make them 'striking' or 'dynamic' in any way but their own. We have tried to let the poet speak for himself, in his own unique way, without imposing upon him our own thoughts or images or ways of speaking. Japanese poetry has its own special quality, one that it is possible to preserve in translation if we proceed with the utmost delicacy and are scrupulous in our interpretation of its movement of thought and image, a movement quite different from that of Western poetry. We feel it is this aspect of Japanese poetry that translators have been unable to convey in their attempts to 'rationalize' the originals in an over-intellectual and analytical way. We think that in these versions readers can hear the poet's own voice speaking, and his thought moving in a Japanese way, which is often distinct from the English way.

Takagi Kyozo was born in Aomori City in 1903. He graduated from a medical university in Manchuria (now in China). He is now an eye specialist in Hirosaki City. He has written a great many poems and short stories, not only in dialect, but in standard Japanese. Prominent among these are *My Requiem* (poems), *The Descendants of Crows* (poems), *Poems that are Not Poems Written by a Poet who is Not a Poet* (poems), *Fengtien Castle and its Neighbourhood* (short stories) and *Three Stories in Dialect* (short stories).

My Way as a Poet

by Takagi Kyozo

MY PROGRESS as a poet can be divided into three stages—the days I sought relief in writing poetry, the days I was lost in a maze, and the days of resignation.

I began writing poetry in 1926 when I was twenty-three years old. After graduating from a higher grade school,[1] I gave up the idea of going on to a university and found employment with a local newspaper. There I happened to meet Kojiro Fukushi,[2] a poet and my fellow provincial. He suggested I write poetry in my own dialect, in accordance with the theory of 'localism' of which he was the leading advocate.

I had begun reading literature in my middle school years, but at that time I had no experience of writing poetry. Furthermore the idea that dialect was dirty and vulgar had preoccupied our thoughts in those days because of the influence of school teaching.

So what exercised my mind after meeting Kojiro Fukushi was how I could write serious literary works in dialect, without vulgarity or folksong naïvety. I believed that if I were to accomplish this aim, I should have to endeavour to instil the highest poetic spirit into my work. As my best model for this purpose I chose from among several poetry magazines I had collected the one called simply *A*[3] edited by Fuyue Anzai[4] and published at Talien in China. I found in this magazine poems that were short and extremely dense, and a new type of prose poems as well.

In 1927, Japan had sunk into the depths of depression. I left the newspaper and went up to Tokyo. But there I was greatly distressed to see the streets filled with the unemployed. Though fortunately I managed to find a position with a small publisher, this firm went bankrupt one year later, and again I was out of work. At last I decided to go to Manchuria and find a position there. In those days I felt that the writing of poetry was my only lifeline—the medium through which I could vent my feelings about my difficult life. So I clung to this lifeline. I often had to put up with criticism

[1] A type of high school that existed under the old educational system. It came between the five years of middle-school and university entrance.

[2] Kojiro Fukushi (1889–1946). His main works are *The Son of the Sun* and *On Ur-Japan*.

[3] Pronounced short as in 'cat'.

[4] Fuyue Anzai (1898–1965). His main works are *The Warship Mari* and *A Salt Lake in Asia*.

9

of dialect poetry, but always Fukushi consoled and encouraged me, saying that one day our poems would be appreciated.

However, even in Manchuria I could not find a job. I entered the Manchuria Medical College in Fengtien. I made my living and school expenses through doing part-time jobs and tutoring. My normal way of life was completely altered, and as a result my poems could not but be filled with reminiscence alone. When my wife died, I stopped writing poetry in dialect. The works written up to that time were collected and published by a friend under the title *Marmelo*.[1] This book was printed, so to speak, to the memory of my dead wife. There was no response to it from the literary world.

Then I entered upon a long, maze-like, zigzag way. Mr. Anzai was still in Talien. He always welcomed me, a poor medical student, and we talked a great deal about poetry. One of the things I was taught by him was the charm of the desert. I came to yearn for the deserts of Central Asia. My usual and favourite method of summoning up poems at that time was to envisage images against the empty spaces of the desert where there was nothing to fix the eye. The poems from those days were collected in *My Requiem*. They are prose poems, and this led me to the writing of novels and short stories.

When the Tokyo magazine to which I contributed my poems ceased publication, I became a member of another group whose leader was Kazuhide Sato.[2] They were publishing a magazine which advocated a new type of fixed-form four-line poem. This gave me a chance to think deeply about poetic rhythm, and to rid myself of Anzai's influence, which was so strong that they used to call me 'the poor man's Anzai'. However, while experimenting with these fixed-form poems, I sensed that something I might call the poetic voice remained the same and could never change. I thought to myself mockingly that 'a crow is a crow after all'. So I published my third book of poems, *The Descendants of Crows*, and stopped writing fixed-form poems.

The Japan–China Incident took place in 1937 and then came the Second World War. At that time I was studying at the university from which I had graduated, as a research student from the local hospital to which I was attached. Communication with mainland Japan became difficult because of the war, so I joined a group of poets in Talien and kept on writing poetry.

[1] A word derived from Portuguese and meaning 'quince'.

[2] Kazuhide Sato (1898–   ). His main works are *Yamato is Beautiful* and *A Collection of New-Rhythm Poems*.

A year after the war ended in 1945 I returned to Japan. By this time I had given up writing poetry completely because I had lost my passion for poetry and because I was discouraged at having had to abandon the manuscripts of many poems when I left Manchuria.

In 1953, to commemorate my fiftieth birthday, I published the second version of *Marmelo*.[1] A local radio station broadcast my reading of the poems. I generated an unexpectedly wide response from listeners. Some declared they had never before realized how beautiful the Tsugaru dialect is, and others even claimed that it sounded very musical. Although the dialect I used in my poems had all but vanished, many people, young people as well, appreciated my poems. It took me more than forty years to see my poems appreciated at their true worth. I was nevertheless encouraged by this development. In Japan, poetry readings were never very popular or common, though the situation may be changing today, so I made the personal discovery for the first time that poems should be heard with the ears, not only read with the eyes.

About that time I first read T. S. Eliot's *The Waste Land* in the translation by Junzaburo Nishiwaki.[2] This poem inspired me so much that once again I felt the desire to write poetry welling up in me. The result is my fourth book of poems entitled *Poems That Are Not Poems By A Poet Who Is Not A Poet*.

Despite my old bones, I am now tackling a long poem whose epigraph is, 'This is the land of death'—after *The Waste Land*. This will be my last book, and, I hope, the culmination of my life's work as a poet.

[1] This is the version (with sonosheet) from which the translations in *The Winter Moon* were made.

[2] Junzaburo Nishiwaki (1894–   ). Main works are *Travellers Do Not Return* and *Modern Allegories*.

1) *Marmelo* (1931). All the poems are written in dialect. This is his most important work.
2) *My Requiem* (1935). Prose poems written in standard Japanese.
3) *The Descendants of Crows* (1939). Poems written in various styles and in standard Japanese.
4) *Fengtien Castle and its Neighbourhood* (1940). Short stories written in standard Japanese. The background of items 2, 3 and 4 is colonial Manchuria under Japanese rule.
5) *Three Stories in Dialect* (1965). In this collection Takagi experimented successfully with writing short stories in Tsugaru dialect.
6) *Poems That Are Not Poems Written By A Poet Who Is Not A Poet* (1965). His most recent poems, written in standard Japanese.
7) *The Old Women's House* (1967). Short stories whose background is Tsugaru, but written in standard Japanese.
8) *A Cluster of Fallen Leaves* (1968). A novel written in standard Japanese Describes the hard life of Japanese repatriates from Manchuria during the period of their repatriation.
9) *Homecoming* (1969). A play.

Besides the above, some twenty short stories and thirty poems were in existence but were lost during the repatriation. He is now writing a long poem and a new novel.

The English translation of the poem 'The Winter Moon' (from *Marmelo*) was first printed in *The Malahat Review* No. 6, 1968. The complete translation of *Marmelo* (English title *The Winter Moon*) appeared in *Japan Quarterly* Vol. XVII, No. 3, 1970 and in *Modern Poetry in Translation* No. 9, 1971. *Transpacific* No. 2 (1969); and *Poetry Australia* Nos. 36/7, 1970 also printed some of his poems. All of these translations are included in this collection, together with many previously unpublished.

Selected Poems

Selected Poems

That's only the willows rustling,
blown by the wind.
Don't cry,
don't cry.
Brides shouldn't cry.
Are you crying because we have no money?
Why did we have to get married in this miserable way?
We can make believe we're playing at houses.

We hold our skinny bodies pressed together,
but get no heat.
Ah, we're like a couple of flies blundering after the sun.
From tomorrow, you'll be going back to the village council-offices again
in purple hakama and black cape, won't you?
Miserable bride and bridegroom!
Don't cry,
don't cry.
There's nothing to be frightened of.
That's only the willows rustling,
blown by the wind.

Sea-Rose
(when I was fourteen)

I thought
I would get my own back on my tormentors.
But I hadn't the guts.
Under the roots of a sea-rose by the
boat-house
I buried my knife and cried.

Ah, the green fruit of the sea-rose tasted sour
as I gazed at the white-crested waves
far out at sea.

Wood Sorrel

For no particular reason
I've been feeling gloomy.
It's not that I don't want to go on living.

The cherry-blossoms have already fallen
under this leaden sky.
On days like these
we think nothing of dying.

I pick some wood sorrel at the side of the lane
and bite it.
The bloom on this flower is
the natural bloom of dust.

O, my twisted mind!
Stones, stepped on, are mute.
If I kept silent,
could I also become a stone?

This wretched life: under the kitchen sink
We can see earth-worms crawling.

Isn't there anyone who
will toss me up into the sky
like a stone?

The Winter Moon

I hit my wife and went out and saw
the moon like ten thousand lanterns.

Over the soft snow after a snowstorm
I am walking with no idea where I am going.

—What is it makes me hate so hard?
When we hate, we are more serious than when we love.
Why now am I starting to feel I love her again?

Everything is like that snowstorm.
When it is over, we see
the moon like a thousand lanterns.

This village has never been
burnished by sun.
The houses,
foundations eaten away by saltwater worms, and
pushed from behind by the high hill,
look as if they're being shoved into the sea.

Look at the hills of Matsumae!
Our village has never been
illumined as beautifully as that.
Everybody in the village is poor
and smells of fish.
The young men hared off somewhere.
Only a lot of old folk with hair like seaweed
stay on here.
Ah, you young lads like dolphins leaping far out to sea—
where did you go?

Sea-shells thrown away and left piled at the roadside, long ago.
Fish-bones, rotting in the earth,
do not grow into trees.

We breathe dense fog from dawn to dusk.
And in the night
we can hear the dead crying out to sea.

This cold rain soon turns to snow.
How meager these rice-shoots!
Yet we have to keep banging an old oil can
to scare off these shrill sparrows.
The sea sounds as if a storm's blowing up.
A flock of seagulls screeching overhead.
A father is reading with vacant eyes a letter from
his daughter working at a cotton-spinning mill.
The mother is trying to make a meal from bruised spuds
she scratched up in the fields.
But the fire will not burn, it only smoulders,
and the matches have all been used.
The house is full of smoke.
The bairn's yelling.
What a miserable evening!

You, flag fluttering at the top of the flagpole!
I am now about to leave for ever
the place where I was born. My ears
are numbed with the wind in this season of thawing snow.
Along the beach, the bare boughs of willows are shivering.
No one has come to see me off.
A distant temple roof gleams with wet.
Ah, this is the town where I was born—
a cradle already grown too narrow for me—
this unlovable town with the ill-natured smile of
a wicked stepmother.

You, fluttering flag!
I am giving up everything now.
But why do I have to force myself to go,
as if I were having to chop off my own hand?
The ship's hooter is blowing.
This is the end of it all.
When the bow turns, I too turn my back on
the place where I was born.
As we get further from the shore
the wind blows stronger.
Oh, you fluttering flag!
Be torn away and flung upon this stormy sea!

Peasant

I blew from my snitch
snot green as rice-pests.

Fisherman

I can't get a look at the girls
for your big backside.

Sleet

A bus.
I ran and shouted.
My paper doll
got all wet and crumpled.

Snowstorm

Children,
hurry up and get to bed.
D'you hear that?
It's a white wolf howling
as he runs round the house.
From a dark corner up in the loft
your dead grandfather and grandmother
are staring at you.
Children,
hurry up and get to bed.

Dawn

I can hear someone pissing.
Is it you, mother?

Through the dense fog
father has come back
with fish-scales all over his body.

'We got a big catch!'

Graveyard

I found it was not
the shadow of some stick
used in the funeral, but
my own long, skinny shade.

The masks of grandpa and grandma lie
beneath the tombstone.
When the wind is blowing,
we can hear them chattering
with toothless gums.

Snow Witch

They are saying that
one evening when big snowflakes were falling
the footprints of the storekeeper's eldest son
came to a stop outside the eating-house.

Next morning they found him hanging
like a broken icicle at the foot of the cliff.

Top

Grandpa was snoring—
so was my spinning top.

Spring

I turned the corner by the barber's and as I went down the back lane

I caught a whiff of baked herring.

Autumn

A dragonfly
on a washing-line for nappies.
(She was married last year.)
The millet stalks—broken skeletons.
Sounds of new cloth being beaten
make my head ache.

Knife

In a stony place
grasshoppers were chirping.
I got a pain in my forehead.

Promises

We pledged our troth by linking little fingers
under the apple blossoms,
but the link broke. She dies.

Seagulls

The sea is stormy;
they can't go out fishing.
Where's your mother?
The bairn's crying in the kitchen.
Why don't you put on the light?

Sallows

Even girls who are not grown up
are powdering their faces now,
hands frostbitten by river water.

They say they are going to town.

Skylark

The colour of the sky I saw from my cradle was
the colour of a halfpenny whistle given me by my mother.

As we walked along the path collecting buds,
turtledoves were cooing.
As we were going down to the swamp to pick the butterbur,
cuckoos were calling.

By the river, where she said yes for the first time,
wild roses were scenting the air.

In the pine grove where I listened to her voice
siskins were warbling.

Alas, now, when those things are all vanishing,
this evening, in the bustle of Tokyo,
I suddenly realize
what she must have been thinking of that day
on our way back from the woods,
as she walked along picking dandelions and
tossing them up in the air.

On the day my sister was married
silverberries in the garden were red as red.

On the day our mother died
a wet snow was falling.

On the day our father died
the ice on the roof had begun to thaw.

On the evening I left home for good
it was the summer fireworks festival.

*Early Spring
at Gappo Park*

This park by the sea where only pine-trees grow
is strangely desolate.
No young girls play here.

Coming out on the beach
we find the east wind blowing hard.

The tang of bottled lemonade
still haunts my tongue.

My friend, sitting on a broken bench,
is telling me dirty stories, but
his voice is snatched
away by the wind.

'Didn't I tell you the marriage would be no good?'
  —That hair ornament got broken.
'There's no use moaning over it now.'
  —Thistles blowing by the white roadside.
'Husband, why don't you say something?'
  —Shower passing over bare hillside fields.
'You needn't come running home to us, daughter.'
  —The coach carries her away behind the pine-grove.

Lightning over Beds of Rice Seedlings

Frogs are croaking, and from time to time
there are flashes of lightning over the beds of rice-seedlings.

She still hasn't come out.

Rain begins to fall.
I'm getting wet to the skin
but I won't budge from here.

The rain's getting heavier,
and the frogs have already stopped croaking.

It seems very late now.
The lights in her house have all been turned off.

Festival Eve

In the front pocket of a baby boy who,
listening to the pipe music,
has sunk into a happy doze
on his nurse's back,
a cardboard pistol and
a few fireworks are getting hot.

Field Fire

Now just after the snow has melted,
in the field next to the pine-grove
children seem to have started a bonfire.
The dead grass has caught fire
and spread its flames.
The children, like the bonfire,
are jumping and cartwheeling.

Stilts

I had been out gathering chickweed leaves
and came home to find
the cage of siskins empty.
The sun was shining all over a warehouse wall, and
I could see the pine-grove in the distance.

The scar left by my fall from my stilts
is still on my kneecap.

Telegraph Pole

In the evenings,
we children would gather round the telegraph pole
on the street corner in front of the chemist's.

The wooden pole would be singing plaintively.
The seal-maker's boy
put his ear to the pole, and
looking at a metal sign advertising medicine for women
told us it was his sister crying in the pole.

Now, twenty years later,
all those children have grown up.
Only I am still crying like that wooden pole,
on the street corner, in the evenings.

Mother

Suddenly I wanted a drink of milk
and I rushed into the house.
Mother was washing her white body
in the dim kitchen.

When I chewed on her breasts,
her milk tasted strangely salty.
(You washed in seawater, didn't you, mother?)

Soon after that, she died,
not long after she had given me her salty milk to drink.

Quince
My wife told me this dream she had when she was dying in Manchuria

I was following a narrow path
through withered grasses
and found in the mud
a fallen quince.
My dead cousin was there too,
eating a rice-ball.
However hard I tried,
I couldn't manage to pick up the fruit.

O, in the village where I was born
it must be snowing now!

A New City

The hotel at dawn filled me with horror.
A smell of mortar was hanging about all the streets.
—I must look for a proper place to live—
Each blast of wind cast rough outlines
of water-towers over canvases of ice.

From behind frozen trees
from behind a dentist's signboard
schoolchildren rushed towards me
waving their skates over their heads like daggers.

I stood at the top of a slope.
Chinese government officials were crowding the square
and crows the sky.

Already I had lost all hope of making my fortune here.

Wind.
National flag in the dust.
Sham street fight.

No fire in the stove
nor in this Russian war-widow.

Is this the day the Mikado's baby was born?

Memorial day commemorating
your country's defeat by mine.

But instead of this, I answered:
The day I was defeated by you.

Then we lay down in the mirror
set in the head of the bed.

Sham street fight.
National flag in the dust.
Wind.

Let's take a look at The Sights of Paris, a 9 mm motion picture.

We're sailing down the Seine.
Marronnier avenues on the other bank of the river.

Gentlemen reading newspapers are walking among rushing taxis and buses.

A poet's statue in the cemetery at Montparnasse.
I am not among those young people laying bunches of flowers on the tomb.

We scamper up the Eiffel Tower.
The Moulin Rouge goes milling round
as night is falling.

Ah! Paris is not with us any more.
Here we are again sipping lukewarm tea in silence.
Outside the thick curtains we can hear the sound of the wind,
of a dusty wind through which the sun glares yellow.

Well, let's run the picture through again
—without rewinding the film.

First we jump off the Eiffel Tower
before dawn is breaking on the Moulin Rouge.
Young people snatch away bunches of flowers from the poet's tomb.
Gentlemen stuff newspapers back in their pockets.
Taxis and buses dash backwards
along marronnier avenues on the other bank of the river.

Now we are sailing up the Seine
and this is the end of the film.

—Paris is not with us any more.

I drove a pony through the dust-storm to reach a patient's home.
But instead of my doctor's bag I found I had taken
one full of catalogues of new motorcar models.
(Those damned Chinese who offered me
pumpkin seeds in the first-class carriage of the Suchow Railway!)

I had to apply my ear right on the Japanese girl's chest.
I had to palpate every bone of her washboard torso
and make my descent into a gloomy cavern
in search of my doctor's bag.

In her delirium she kept on saying
she wanted to see again the waters of Japan.
To my ear, her heart sounded distinctly
like an ebbing tide.

So without any further ado I was able
to diagnose tuberculosis.
I was handicapped by the loss of my bag, and soon,
before I could do anything for her, she died.

When I left the house, I found my pony was missing.
I staggered through the storm of dust,
holding under one arm the bag
full of catalogues of new motorcars.

I kept thinking of the long coastline of Japan,
still puzzling over what had become of my bag.

The view of the International Settlement
seen through a periscope
might be recommended for inclusion in the new design
of bank notes in the Republic of China.
Russian maidens in black swimsuits are
camouflaged Q-ships.
Sailors who declined the Order of the Crimson Starfish
are transformed into white foam and
wash overboard from their ships.
I pick up an opium pipe from under a gyroscope
and recall the phosphorescence
in the wake of a torpedo our ship was tracking.
However, because I forgot the signals
to be used at sea in contacting our mother ship,
this evening too, the Scorpion violates
the sextant's centre, and
the keel of the old ship writhes in agony
in mud and seaweed.
I take off my life-jacket and give the order:
'Verify with depth-gauge angle of descent of rust-red morale!'

'What's the matter with this ship?'
The ship hasn't moved an inch
though sailing time has already passed.

'I suppose they can't find the Blue Peter,'
answered the doctor, mixing
a draught of medicine for my stomach.

'It wouldn't be this, would it?'
I extracted from my trouser pocket
a blue-hemmed snotrag stinking of petrol
that I picked off the deck a while before.

The doctor, smiling, got up and opened the porthole.
We could see a cloudy sky
floating above the skin of the ocean.

Then I started to wipe my shoes, slowly,
with the blue cloth.

Sleep

Falling asleep at night is training for diving into death
—a dive we make wearing pyjamas.

After only a momentary hesitation we plunge headlong
Then float up, leaving a white wake of dreams.

So when we die
We can dive confidently into the pit of death.

Day of Metamorphosis

The sun glares.
The road is white.
The clouds are gradually coming to the boil.
The wind is already chill.
Along the concrete wall
My shadow goes crawling.
I find an exhausted butterfly in my path.

In this scene turned inside out,
I shall walk like an evangelist
Listening to faint, far-off thunders.

Song of One Possessed

At dusk in the bustle of a town
I mouth meaningless words
And stagger along like one possessed.
The windows of houses are already lighted.
—Why don't you go home?

What kind of spell these words leaking from your parched lips?
No. They are all my old poems—
The songs of my perished youth.

How can I expect practical folk to listen to these songs?
They only feel suspicious of my strange appearance.

Ah! My songs have foundered under that muddy sky.
They are all stones by the roadside, or horse droppings.

Yet, on the back of a bony donkey,
I sing:
'Still a faint radiance in the west!'

A Fancy Dress Party

First I was caught by ugly Queen Victoria (who, I found,
    was the wife of a chaplain to the British Consul).
While I was clasping this old queen's body in
    my arms, I remembered what I was
told by my dancing teacher (who was also an old lady):
    When you are dancing with an elderly woman, you must
never wear a martyred expression on your face.
    So I crucified this old queen in the shadow of a palm tree.

I shall append my signature to each of my wedding invitations.
My name, brushed in Chinese fashion, is a black spider crawling over red
    paper.
Soon the khans of the twenty-five Mongolian tribes will be accepting my
    invitation
and will come post-haste on the backs of camels bearing man-made furs
    and jade.
  I pray that we shall have bad weather on my wedding day.
  While I busy myself estimating the value of the presents and weighing
out the dinner provisions for my guests, who will be arriving covered with
yellow dust, my manservant sensitively selects a Stravinsky record.
  I brandish a baton furiously in front of the big gramophone.

THIS PRIVATE, like others, was sometimes sent comfort kits from unknown women when he was on service in the field. In every kit, he would find a tablet of scented soap, of the brand called 'Angel'. He accumulated quite a number of tablets. So he thought he would send them to his old mother, who liked this brand very much. But by the time he had collected a dozen cakes of the soap, he had to go to the front. On the night before a full-scale attack was to be launched, he was ordered to carry out sentry duties. He felt sorry he had missed the chance to send the cakes of soap to his old mother. He stood listening to the twelve angels flapping their wings, and staring at the dark horizon.

Then, suddenly, twelve cakes of soap loomed up from beyond the horizon. Soon they had formed a square, and then they deployed. The cakes of soap came nearer and nearer and made straight for him. Before he had time to see what they really were, gunfire flashed right under his nose. Before he could take aim with his rifle, he was knocked to the ground. Then silence. The twelve angels took wing from around his dead body, and flew quietly away into the black night, leaving behind them a whiff of scented soap.

As there are in this world funny things that are not funny things,
so in this city that is not a city there is day that is not day and night that is
    not night.
Gambling that is not gambling goes on and
murders that are not murders keep getting done every day.
Look!
A husband who is not a husband and a wife who is not a wife
take a child who is not a child, go for a walk along a street that is not a
    street,
have a meal that is not a meal, drink rice wine that is not rice wine and get
    drunk,
shout Japanese that is not Japanese, and in the end
start a quarrel that is not a quarrel.

Old women who are not old women make their toilet that is not a toilet,
wear on their faces smiles that are not smiles,
and come swinging their hips.
People engage in trades that are not trades.
Psychopaths who are not psychopaths carry in their pockets weapons that
    are not weapons and go walking up and down.
The rich who are not rich spend recklessly money that is not money.
Animals that are not animals go on living lives that are not life.
Beggars that are not beggars come up asking for money:
  'All you passing by! Please make a donation!
  All you in the streets! Please support our cause!'

As there are in this world serious things that are not serious things,
so there are rivers that are not rivers and land that is not land.
Politicians who are not politicians take part in politics that is not politics.
Government officials who are not government officials sink into corruption
    that is not corruption.
Teachers who are not teachers provide education that is not education,
bring up human beings who are not human beings.
Patients who are not patients take medicines that are not medicines.
Believers who are not believers worship the god who is no god.

Men of culture who are not men of culture talk of culture that is not culture.
Military men who are not military men ride tanks that are not tanks and
     warships that are not warships
and demand the purchase of fighter planes that are not fighter planes.
One day you will see!
The army that is not an army will gather up its courage that is not courage,
go to war that is not a war, put an end to its lives that are not lives,
and begin once more its deaths that are not deaths.
  'All you passing by! Please make a donation!
  All you in the streets! Please support our cause!'

If you push a button
a door opens

  you push a button
it is light even at night

    push a button
you make a nonstop trip to the 100th floor

      push   button
you get a meal

      pu   button
you hear music

      p   button
the world's news becomes available

        button
our activities are photographed and our words are recorded

        but
the police are called out

        bu
a patrol car appears

          b
we vanish

'Full up. Take the next one.'
Buses. Commuter trains. Cheap bars. Cinemas. Cabarets.
Restaurants in department stores. Houses of assignation for young couples
    and day trippers.
Government-built housing.
    All full up!

Maternity hospitals. Nursery schools for babies and infants. Kindergartens.
Primary schools. Junior and senior high schools. Public and private uni-
    versities.
Employment agencies. Prisons. Old people's homes. Hospitals.
Crematoriums. Public cemeteries.
    All full up!
    That's the lot!

So now seems to be the time to say goodbye.
Goodbye, friends, my children, my wife.
I turn my back on the lot of you.
Where a snowdrift ends
a funeral procession passes on.

'OFF LIMITS'
Here I have come to get rid of myself.
I am made naked.
Ah . . . What a world this is!
Birds do not sing here.
Even earthworms are nowhere to be seen.
No sun.
No storms.
What silence!
I see only frozen fields in a faint dimness.

I will go fearlessly.

That winter
the rats all died.
Early one spring afternoon
I go out into the parched streets.
Sunlight, reflected in the display windows of a department store,
pierces my forehead.
Disabled war veterans hold out empty tins.
    —please—please—
I spit from the bridge at the dirty surface of a narrow river.
On the water I see someone's face.
It's that guy.

The radio stuck in a tobacco kiosk
broadcasts an all-in wrestling match,
shouts: He's dragged him into a corner and is wringing his neck!

In the garden of an old people's home
old people sitting in a row like dried fish.
A hearse dashes out of the entrance.
The queue outside the hospital does not move.
They are going to sell their blood.
Lots of faces appear and hands are waved
at the broken windows of a mental patients' ward.

As the townscapes split
and the rice-fields squeeze in
the air is gradually getting more and more parched.
Vapour rises from a rubbish tip.
Crows are kicking up a fuss.
There that guy is squatting.

At dusk
chairs are shoved out of place all over the room
and strangers are seen sitting down.
Flowers picked this morning
are withering on a sheet of newspaper.

My friends, I must go.
That guy is waiting.
—He is standing behind the door, with his back to me.
I rush down the stairs
and walk around in the dusty wind,
feeling at my back his footsteps dogging me.

The red tail-lamp of an express train
is swallowed up by the snowstorm.
It was seen off only by
a luggage van
abandoned on a siding
in a lonely station.

As the night advances
and the storm ceases
and all creatures hold their breath,
the stars in a clear winter sky
exchange signals with the lights of villages.
Soon the stars dance down, one by one.
The luggage van covered with snow,
masquerading as a black-robed priest,
offers a silent prayer
on this holy intercourse
between sky and earth.

Beneath our feet
the earth rotates.
It's not that we have fancy footwork,
it's just the earth rotating that bears us on.

But what's all this balancing on a ball?
I am rather tired of it.
   Stop playing the clown;
   nobody claps.
A rope ladder is hanging from the ceiling.
It is swaying before us.
Soon we shall have to put on a show of jumping at it.
The hour may come today.
Even if we succeed,
no one applauds.

   Don't loiter on your way.
   —the road is zigzag.
Don't take your eyes off the road.
—there are many distractions around us.
Look out!
There's a hole in the road.

When my turn comes,
I ask the band to play
'Paradise and Hell.'
I throw off my pierrot's costume
and kick at the earth
so as to take a big leap through the air.
If only I manage to catch the end of the rope—
   'Got it!'
   'Well, good-bye, all.'
Then someone hauls my body up.
I can sleep tight in the actors' room in the attic.

—Is there nobody here?
—Nobody who knows you and nobody you know
have come here to meet you.

In the next room
a man and a woman are merrily
talking and laughing,
among a rattle of cups and dishes.
Outside the window
spring sunlight is bright.

—Is there nobody here?
—The play has just finished.
On the dark stage
a big curtain is swaying heavily,
blown by a wind from the trapdoor.
Stage direction: He is expressionless and exits.
—No one here?
—There are no human beings.

The earth, on which all creatures are dying out,
goes on rotating as before.